FROM THERE:
SOME THOUGHTS ON
POETRY & PLACE

OTHER BOOKS BY
STEPHEN BURT

Belmont, Graywolf, 2013

The Art of the Sonnet, with David Mikics, Harvard UP, 2010

Close Calls with Nonsense: Reading New Poetry, Graywolf, 2009

The Forms of Youth: 20th-Century Poetry and Adolescence, Columbia UP, 2007

Parallel Play, Graywolf, 2006

Randall Jarrell and His Age, Columbia UP, 2002

From There: Some Thoughts on Poetry & Place

THE 2015 GARNETT SEDGEWICK MEMORIAL LECTURE

Stephen Burt

RONSDALE PRESS
VANCOUVER, BC

FROM THERE: SOME THOUGHTS ON POETRY & PLACE

RONSDALE PRESS
3350 West 21st Avenue, Vancouver, B.C. Canada V6S 1G7
www.ronsdalepress.com

Typesetting: Julie Cochrane, in Minion 11 on 15
Cover Design: Julie Cochrane
Paper: Ancient Forest Friendly Husky 60 lb., FSC Recycled, 100% post-consumer waste, totally chlorine-free and acid-free.

Ronsdale Press wishes to thank the following for their support of its publishing program: the Canada Council for the Arts, the Government of Canada through the Canada Book Fund, the British Columbia Arts Council, and the Province of British Columbia through the British Columbia Book Publishing Tax Credit program.

Canada Council for the Arts Conseil des arts du Canada Funded by the Government of Canada Financé par le gouvernement du Canada Canada BRITISH COLUMBIA ARTS COUNCIL An agency of the Province of British Columbia

Library and Archives Canada Cataloguing in Publication

Burt, Stephen, 1971–, author
From there: some thoughts on poetry and place / Stephen Burt.

(The 2015 Garnett Sedgewick memorial lecture)
Includes bibliographical references.
Issued in print and electronic formats.
ISBN 978-1-55380-461-1 (print)
ISBN 978-1-55380-462-8 (ebook) / ISBN 978-1-55380-463-5 (pdf)

1. English poetry—History and criticism. 2. Canadian poetry (English)—History and criticism. 3. Landscapes in literature. 4. Geographical perception in literature. 5. Time in literature. 6. Place attachment. I. Title. II. Series: Garnett Sedgewick memorial lecture

PR508 L35 B87 2016 821.009'358 C2015-907053-8 C2015-907054-6

At Ronsdale Press we are committed to protecting the environment. To this end we are working with Canopy and printers to phase out our use of paper produced from ancient forests. This book is one step towards that goal.

Printed in Canada by Island Blue, Victoria, B.C.

ACKNOWLEDGEMENTS

My thanks to the University of British Columbia and its English Department for the great honor of delivering the 2015 Sedgewick Lecture; my thanks in particular to Leslie Arnovick, Stephen Guy-Bray, and Stephen Partridge, who did so much to bring me to B.C., and also to Elise Partridge, who inspired my wish to visit B.C. more than ten years ago: I wish I could have come to see her there. I also wish to thank Paul Chafe, Steve Kistulentz, Jennifer Lewin, Christopher Ricks, and my colleagues James Engell and James Simpson for soliciting or responding, sometimes in earlier versions, to parts of what became the lecture delivered at UBC.

INTRODUCTION

The first Sedgewick Lecture was given in 1955, six years after Dr. Sedgewick's death. Since then, the lecture has been given (almost) annually and has featured many leading scholars, including most recently, Jonathan Gil Harris, Deborah Cameron, and Fred Wah. In 2015, the lecture was given by Stephen Burt of Harvard University.

The lectures are named after Garnett G. Sedgewick, the first head of the Department of English at the University of British Columbia. Dr. Sedgewick was hired by UBC in 1918 and became head in 1920; he served as head until 1948. He laid the foundation for the department and presided over the beginnings of its rapid expansion after World War II. Dr. Sedgewick was also a noted Shakespearean, an acclaimed teacher, and a columnist in the *Vancouver Sun*.

In 2015, we were very fortunate to have Stephen Burt as the Sedgewick Lecturer. Dr. Burt is professor of English at Harvard University, where he specializes in contemporary poetry and poetics. He also has interests in the contemporary arts more generally. He has published widely in these fields. His most notable books are perhaps *The Art of the Sonnet* (co-written with David Mikics) and *Close Calls with Nonsense: Reading New Poetry*.

As well as establishing himself as one of the most consistently interesting and perceptive critics of new and frequently experimental American poetry, Dr. Burt is a distinguished poet in his own right. He also publishes in a variety of venues on comics, graphic novels, science fiction, music, and increasingly on gender. In all these areas, he has used his considerable intellect and his distinctive style to great effect and has established an idiosyncratic and valuable voice. His Sedgewick Lecture was a wide-ranging and entertaining look at a number of issues in contemporary poetry and was a great hit with everyone.

Dr. Burt was suggested for the lecture by my colleague Stephen Partridge and by his wife Elise Partridge, who was herself a very successful poet. I am sorry to report that Elise died before the lecture. Fittingly, Dr. Burt dealt with some of her poems in his lecture. I would like to dedicate this book to her memory.

— Stephen Guy-Bray
Professor and Head

FROM THERE: SOME THOUGHTS ON POETRY & PLACE

Those of us who study poetry have got used to hearing — some of us have even got used to saying — that poetry, or lyric poetry, or modern lyric poetry, imagines a speaking self outside space and time: that while you are reading a poem, it does not matter who or where you are. In lyric, writes Helen Vendler, "the human being becomes a set of warring passions independent of time and space. . . . Insofar as the typical lyric exists only in the here and now it exists nowhere" (5). The soul or the self or the "I" in lyric poetry must turn its circumstances and its worldly origins into trope, or cast them aside: that is what Allen Grossman appeared to mean when he wrote that "the artistic gesture must be departicularized in order to obtain its efficacy *for another*" (267–68). And it is what W. B. Yeats appeared to mean when he wrote, "All that is personal soon rots; it must be packed in ice or salt," for transport, as it were, away from its point of origin in time and space (*Essays* 509). To Brian Boyd, "Lyric poetry allows us the illusion of access to another's thought at its least constrained by circumstance, in the very act of appealing to others regardless of *their* circumstances" (29). The contemporary poet and essayist Dan Beachy-Quick agrees: for him, "the poem functions on the page as a location that ceases to be a location. The poem on the page . . . does not make a distinct place *in* the world, nor does it make a distinct place *of* the world" (7).

Famous poems throughout the history of English (and not only English) also appear to insist on their own independence from time and space, hence from place, from any really existing environment. Think of Shakespeare: "So long as men can breathe, or eyes can see,/ So long lives this, and this gives life to thee." Think of Richard Lovelace's most often quoted poem, "To Althea, From Prison," where "Stone walls do not a prison make,/ Nor iron bars a cage": the poetic spirit sings freely from any, or from no place. Think of A. E. Housman, whose thoroughly traditional (and immediately, enduringly popular) lyric poems insist on their commonality with readers across time and space: "Others, I am not the first,/ Have willed more mischief than they durst:/ If in the breathless night I too/ Shiver now, 'tis nothing new" (47) (I will come back to Housman). Think of Adrienne Rich's anthology piece "Power," in which the poem itself and the wisdom the poem brings — "Her wounds came from the same source as her power" — are like a glass bottle, a message in a bottle, recovered at least decades after it was lost (33). Or think of

A. E. Housman (1859–1936)

Walt Whitman (to whom I will also return) declaring "It avails not neither time or place — distance avails not" (308). Whitman is always promising to reach you, his anointed reader, across time and space, and in that promise (however grandly unusual his other promises) he is hardly alone.

And yet when we start looking for claims — in poems and in prose — about lyric poems' independence from time and space we can find the opposite claims too, and pretty easily, whether we look in the Renaissance, or in the nineteenth century, or among modernists, or right now. Rich's poem "Power" envisions that message from Curie, or the message about Curie, recovered by a backhoe, digging into the Earth. Rich's even more famous poem "Diving Into the Wreck" requires us to imagine a site underwater: "I came to explore the wreck. . . . The words are maps" (15). It is poetry as archaeology, a model if not a method that resonates with such partisans of literal site-specificity as Charles Olson, whose Gloucester poems Rich certainly knew, and with contemporary poets as distant from Olson methodologically as Seamus Heaney and Stanley Kunitz (as in Kunitz's poem "The Layers"). One of Housman's best poems tells us that he and you and I and a Roman soldier have felt the same way, that the most basic units of feeling are independent of history, but it can only come to that conclusion — Housman only experiences that solidarity as an intuitively right conclusion — because Housman's Shropshire lad and his Roman soldier have been standing in and contemplating the same place:

> Then, 'twas before my time, the Roman
> At yonder heaving hill would stare:
> The blood that warms an English yeoman,
> The thoughts that hurt him, they were there.
>
> There, like the wind through woods in riot,
> Through him the gale of life blew high;
> The tree of man was never quiet:
> Then 'twas the Roman, now 'tis I. (48)

That famous line of Whitman's about how time and place do not matter comes from a poem whose place surely does matter, "Crossing Brooklyn Ferry": "Just as you feel when you look on the river and sky, so I felt" (309).

Theorists of poetry, too — including lyric poetry, whatever the term means to each theorist who uses it — have often said that the best poems preserve connections to real places where people can live. We expect those sorts of claims from Olson, and from Olson's friend Robert Creeley, who wrote in 1962: "No matter what becomes of it, art is local, local to a place and to a person, or group of persons. . . . It happens somewhere, not everywhere" (484). We expect such claims as well from William Carlos Williams: "From the shapes of men's lives imparted by the places where they have experience, good writing springs" (*Selected Essays* 132). Williams kept trying to prove as much in his own poems, too: "Spirit of place rises from these ashes/ repeating secretly an obscure refrain:// This is my house and here I live" (*Collected Poems Volume I*, 461).

And yet it would be a terrific mistake to ascribe an interest in place, in site, in location as a ground for lyric poetry, only to the so-called New Americans, to moderns who wanted to follow (or who were) Williams, or to the contemporary poets — from Daphne Marlatt in Vancouver to the wonderful Ian Wedde in Auckland — who fashioned their poetry in those modernists' image. It was W. H. Auden who wrote that poets "hope to be,/ like some valley cheese,/ local, but prized elsewhere" (353). Where would T. S. Eliot be without his "certain half-deserted streets," without the London (not to mention "Jerusalem Athens Alexandria") whose streets and churches inform *The Waste Land*, or without the locales around which he built *Four Quartets*? You can turn almost anywhere in the last two centuries and find the idea — I quote the English poet and critic Neil Powell, whose sympathies are certainly not New American — that "culture, and literary culture especially, depends on local roots; as in gardening, these roots are transplantable with care, but they mustn't be . . . completely severed" (7). Henry Wadsworth Longfellow spent

T. S. Eliot (1888–1965)

his last decade compiling a mammoth anthology — it ran to thirty-one volumes — called *Poems of Places*, aspiring to reprint, in English, some piece of verse about every location on Earth. "In Longfellow's collection," writes his best critic, Christoph Irmscher, "places are texts and can be accessed by anyone who is capable of turning the page" (202). You can find a similar endeavor today, on the Internet, thanks to the intrepid editors of poetryatlas.com: "Everywhere on Earth has a poem written about it," the landing page contends. "We collect any poem written about a place, whether by great poets, or by you."

This aspiration to cover the world with poetry, or if you prefer to honor its diversity of locales, goes back a very long way. Poems from every period of English verse describe particular places, from battlefields and estates to sites within London (see Mark Ford's anthology *London*). After the success of John Denham's "Cooper's Hill," as Samuel Johnson later complained, eighteenth-century poets "left scarcely a corner of the island not dignified by either rhyme or blank verse" (93). But the descriptions have not always worked the same way. Fiona Stafford has shown how Romantic-period poets identified their work with particular places, with "local attachments," especially places far from the national capital, in part thanks to the example of Burns. "The phenomenal success of Robert Burns," Stafford writes, "demonstrated that poems rooted firmly in an identifiable region might present an invigorating challenge to neo-classical assump-

Robert Burns (1759–1796)

tions" (20). It was a challenge that William Wordsworth, in particular — the man who wrote "Poems on the Naming of Places" — took up: and it was in the Romantic period, for Stafford, that "local detail . . . began to seem essential to art with any aspiration to permanence" (30). "Local poetry" — by Burns and Wordsworth, Scott and others — "was playing an important psychological role in emphasizing possible connections to a body whose existence extended beyond that of the individual" (90).

I think she is right about local poetry in her period, though (as I will suggest) some earlier as well as much later poetry seeks what might be surprisingly similar effects. It's not news to say that one or another poet or group of poets has tried to make a sense of place central: there are now bodies of critical work, careers, organized around the claim that certain poets and groups respond to their place. In particular, you can see this claim made for 18th-century prospect poetry: for Burns; for Wordsworth; for John Clare; for Charles Olson (who never tired of making it himself); for writers of contemporary book-length, ecologically minded poems about watersheds or metropolitan areas, such as Alice Oswald in England, Peter O'Leary in the American Midwest, and John Kinsella in western Australia; and for many participants in the last half-century of British "alternative," avant-garde, or neo-modernist poetry, beginning with Roy Fisher's Birmingham and Basil Bunting's Northeast (Neal Alexander and David Cooper have recently examined that last set of claims).

Without contradicting any of those arguments, I want to show — what I think none of them show — both how and why they overlap: how often, and why, many apparently dissimilar kinds and modes of poetry, literally across the English-speaking world, claim to be, or at least support claims that they *might* be, responsive to the spirit of some place. I will then try to distinguish between notions of place, some immediate, some more abstracted and larger in scope; and I will try to persuade you to see particular virtues and modes of representing place in particular modern poets and poems.

Before I show that, I want to note — I'll come back to it later on — how many overlapping or concentric, but far from coterminous, meanings we give the word "place." D. H. Lawrence, who did much to popularize the term "spirit of place," sometimes used it to mean the spirit of a continent: it might also mean a town, or a city block. Not only do various poets have various catchment areas when they take up, embody in verse, the spirit of a place; what they mean by place affects the kind of verse technique that they can use.

Why are there so many otherwise dissimilar poems about places? Why so many places, so close to the hearts of these poems? Because it asks us to extrapolate scenes and mentalities from particular, relatively short pieces of language, because it asks us to imagine a voice or an implied creator, and an inward life for that creator, poetry can let us see with apparently new eyes some place that we already know, let us re-inhabit places we knew long ago — "Heavens, I recognize the place, I know it!" in Elizabeth Bishop's words — or evoke places we have never actually seen (165). And these goals overlap: the same poem can do all three things for three different readers, and thus bring those readers closer together. What a hostile reader might dub armchair travel became for Henry Wadsworth Longfellow one of the goals that poems exist to serve. "Just as he conflates the near and the far," writes Irmscher, *Poems on Places* "removes all constraints of time and allows a dialogue . . . between the most unlikely of interlocutors, writers long dead and writers still alive" (211–12). What do those interlocutors share? Some interest in the same place. The same thing happens when we read "Crossing Brooklyn Ferry" — if not when we read "Cooper's Hill."

It seems now as if we can say both that we expect poems to take us away from real time and real space, and that widely admired poems from several periods and traditions do the reverse: they start in and point back to and tell us that they depend on a place, often a real place with geographical features and a proper noun for a name. Is there a contradiction here? If not, where might we find an explanation? One explanation might double as a dismissal. Poems are about all sorts of things, places included, but we expect poems about places to be (also) without place, outside place and time, because we live in a time when we expect every poem to be "lyric," to take place outside place and time. That expectation comes to us thanks to what Virginia Jackson and Yopie Prins call "lyricization," and it creates a non-problem, a category mistake, when we think about older, or about New American, or about other site-specific poems (2).

That's one explanation, but it's insufficient, even if Jackson's full argument about "lyricization" is true (and I think it is not). The very same poems that tell us they are connected to a place, take their strength from a place, are often the same poems that tell us, *within the poem*, that their figures and feelings transcend space and time: some of these poems even tell us that their portrayals of place are what allow the poet's past self to communicate with a present self, or with us, in the poet's future. So in "Lines Composed a Few Miles Above Tintern Abbey," and so also in Williams's New Jersey (I think here of his poem "The Forgotten City," though you'll have your own favorite), so in Wallace Stevens's Connecticut, so in Elizabeth Bishop's Ouro Preto and Cape Breton and Santarém, so in T. S. Eliot, in parts of *The Waste Land*, and clearly in *Four Quartets*.

So even in Juliana Spahr, whose recent collection of poems and poetic prose *Well Then There Now* examines our frustrated or frustrating, culpable or colonial or laudable or sustainable — but in any case apparently inescapable — wish to believe we belong in the place where we live, to believe that — as Robert Frost put it — "we were the land's." Spahr, of white Anglo working-class Appalachian descent, wrote much of *Well Then There Now* in Hawai'i, where she did not feel she could belong. The first part of *Well Then There Now* reinterprets and disassembles Frost's famous (or infamous) sonnet "The Gift Outright": "Some of we and the land that was never ours while we were the land's. Started from us and the ground which was never with we while we were the ground. Some of we wore the land. Some of we carried the ground. Some of we planted grapes" (12). "Power," Spahr observes in the same book, "clusters in close patterns on top of geography" (41). Her poetry tries to show where power works, and why it ends up there. But it also pursues her frustrated desire to inhabit the spaces, past or present, where she has lived, especially the parts that look polluted or prosaic, unfit for other kinds of poems, like much of her own hometown, Chillicothe, Ohio: "It was a brackish stream and it went through the field beside our house./ But we let it into our hearts the brackish parts of it also" (130).

Spahr's poetry, as canny as it becomes about belonging, about citizenship, about how power shapes our impressions of lived-in places, almost always tells us what it is trying to do. Other poets of place can be more circumspect. Lorine Niedecker's "Lake Superior" has just been republished with supporting documents showing how it draws its facts from Niedecker's automobile tour of northern Wisconsin, Ontario and Minnesota. Much of that almost teasingly bare poem makes clipped verse out of local history, but its last components must count as lyric:

> The smooth black stone
> I picked up in true source park
>   the leaf beside it
> once was stone
>
> Why should we hurry
>   Home
>
>   *
>
> I'm sorry to have missed
>   Sand Lake
> My dear one tells me
>   we did not
> We watched a gopher there (*Lake Superior* 6)

Notice how when Niedecker dwells on a place, when she slows her lines down, seems to concentrate on the place, she ends up making connections, mending missed connections, in time: the smooth stone, the "true source" (of the St. Croix River), becomes a substitute for the merely personal "home," whose memories cannot contain the experience that the poet has tried to set down.

That use of "we" (both "my partner and I" and "you and I") in describing the visit, the place, seems paradigmatic: but before we can see why, we should go back in time. When did place start to seem important in lyric poems (or, if you prefer, in song-like poems that condense strong emotion)? Locodescriptive poetry has been important in English since "Cooper's Hill" became a late 17th-century model, with precedents even before that in country-house poetry, and in poems (often satirical) about London. Locodescriptive poetry merged with the poetry of strong personal feeling — with "lyrical" work, if you like, or with sentiment — no later than in the mid-18th century, with sonnets by Thomas Warton, with Thomas Gray, and then with Charlotte Smith.

From then on one of the standard ways to write a very personal, and yet figurative, "lyrical" poem, was to stand in a place and let the place stand for the person, the outward geography for the inner life: thus "Lines Composed a Few Miles Above Tintern Abbey," "Frost at Midnight," "Crossing Brooklyn Ferry," "Dover Beach," "Two in the Campagna," "The Whitsun Weddings" (where the place is first a train platform, then London), or "San Sepolcro," or "Meditation at Lagunitas," or "For the Union Dead," or most of the best-known poems by Elizabeth Bishop, James Wright, Richard Hugo, Frank O'Hara, Langston Hughes (who names places in Harlem), by Rae Armantrout (whose poems are full of San Diego, though she does not name streets), and those are only U.S. and U.K. poets: readers familiar with Toronto or with Port-of-Spain will supply other examples. That is the way of writing poetry that Spahr's essays and catalogs and self-interrogating longer poetic forms consider and try to reject, and, arguably, sometimes, accept. Other diverse aspects of human experience have not been "covered" by poetry in the same way: you probably cannot find a decent poem for every possible article of clothing, for example, or for every significant food.

Scene at the ferry landing in Brooklyn, as depicted in Ballou's Pictorial, *1857.*

Why not? Why should place matter more? Here is one reason: the experience of a place allows people to literally come together, to meet each other where we are. (That is what happens in Spahr's poems when she uses, very self-consciously, not "I," but "we.") Lyric or quasi-lyric poems about place become evidence for the meeting of outside and inside, the manifestation of what's "inside" you to the "outside" of other people, that we may want lyric poetry to provide. They bring — to use Rilke's terms, or Randall Jarrell's — a "soul" (*Seele*), a "raw thing," a "being inside," into "space" (*Raum*), an occupied and extensive world (39). One of the reasons, though not the only reason, that Pound's *Pisan Cantos* seems to so many of us like the best part of Pound's long poem has to do with its ability to return to a particular place, a place that stays constant (like a tonic chord) no matter where else in time, space, style or tone the poem tries to go. It is not, of course, a pleasant place: it's a cage. "If the hoarfrost grip thy tent/ Thou wilt give thanks when night is spent" (540). The *Pisan Cantos* permit themselves to be read (as the *Cantos* in general cannot be read) as meditative locodescriptive lyric, even as a Greater Romantic Ode: Pound lingers, remembering, while "A fat moon rises lop-sided over the mountain." Of course, like "To Althea," the "Pisan Cantos" are prison poetry too: "at my grates no Althea" (519).

This succession of meditative locodescriptive works (whether or not we call them all "lyric") has been attacked on the grounds that it lets the imperial self rule the landscape, that it doesn't respect the otherness of the not-I, the human or non-human other. This critique first gathered force not around the idea of "place" in general but around "landscape" as a pictorial and poetic genre, as in the work of John Barrell. Bonnie Costello, among other critics, has defended "landscape poetry" against this critique, and Spahr — among others — responds directly to it; the poems about landscapes, of "I" and not "we" in a name place, make up a stream, over several generations, that Charles Altieri tried to dam up in the 1980s, declaring the exhaustion of a sub-genre he named "the scenic poem."

Yet it survives, and not just because poets are lazy. Why do we go back to scenes, to senses of places, whether our tastes are more like Pound's, or Marlatt's, or Robert Frost's? Why do we keep finding places when we seek ourselves, or what we want to believe are other people's selves? And why do we keep on taking a kind of poem that starts from and goes back to a scene, a description of place, as an ideal-typical form for poetry, or for modern poetry, or for modern lyric poems? Why does that assumption — that poems start from places, and return to places — recur among poets whom we think have not much in common — Eliot and Olson, for example, or (as Lytle Shaw has shown) Amiri Baraka and Gary Snyder, or James Merrill and the Pisan Pound?

Maybe because these poems do with their geography what we most often, most strongly now want poetry in general (now that we expect it to be "lyric" poetry) to do: we want it to make the words that we can find "out there," in the verifiable world, available as tropes, as a version of somebody's inner life, "in here," to make them present to somebody else at some other time. Indeed the best-known poems — and not just contemporary poems — about literal places often describe that process of finding, of realizing that somebody else has been here before, not only "here" in a physical place but also "here" in a psychic situation like (if not identical to) one's own. If you want a clearly lyrical example of this effect — call it the "Crossing Brooklyn Ferry" effect — long before Whitman, try Dorigen's song in Chaucer's "Franklin's Tale" (lines 857–94). She sings that she was not the first, and will not be the last, to decry the sight of "theese grisly feendly rokkes blake": "An hundred thousand bodyes of mankynde/ Han rokyes slain, al they be nat in mynd. . . . This rokkes sleen myn herte for the feere" (216; ll. 868, 877–78, 893). If you know the tale, you know that Dorigen's exemplary fidelity turns out to be stronger, and longer-lasting, than the defining features of her physical place, which disappear — but will then reappear — under the waves.

Someone like me has felt as I feel, here, before, and someone like me will come here and feel that way again: That's the frequent burden of Housman's Shropshire lyrics (set in a county where Housman had never lived): Housman's lad feels and shows that he feels what the Roman soldier felt even though "Today the Roman and his trouble/ Are ashes under Uricon." "Crossing Brooklyn Ferry" incorporates the same effect — you know me and know something of how I feel because, though we live at different times and under different circumstances, we see the same place. Whitman relies on the place, on sense of place, as evidence. And it is evidence supported by technique. Whitman's long lines, reaching out as if to take your hand, don't sound like Housman's end-stopped, almost automatically memorizable quatrains, but the poems use their differing aural

Walt Whitman (1819–1892)

means to similar affective ends. And it's an effect (look, traveler, *siste, viator*, here you are too) that we can find, once we look for it, in poems (including Chaucer's) famous before the Romantics were born.

Once we see place, and the sense of place, in poetry as a way of doing the work that we want lyric to do — connecting the "out there" to the "in here"; connecting the interior life that can only be mine to the tangible, visible, or socially acknowledged universe that could be yours as well — we can also see, and we are about to see, how a few contemporary poets use the various features of poetry to inhabit and to present a real place (I'll focus on two, C. D. Wright and Mary Dalton, with a few more poets considered quickly in between). We might also see why lyric poetry has kept up a special relationship to certain kinds of places, among them prisons, homes, and graveyards: and we can see how the various features that poems possess — diction, syntax, line shape, and the like — establish different relationships to different aspects of the sense of place.

C. D. Wright grew up in the Ozarks and began writing as a student at the University of Arkansas-Fayetteville; her experience there has marked her reception and her subsequent career, including a few book-length poems. She has also compiled geographical anthologies and multimedia projects, such as *A Walk-in Book of Arkansas* (1994). To see her consider location as the basis for short poems — for lyric, for epigram, for musical fragment, for the miniaturized ode — we need to look at only one book, *String Light* (1991), whose poems cohere around slang and scenes and properties of their Arkansas place. When Wright imagines herself, like Whitman, speaking to the remote future — "I am your ancestor," she writes — she sees herself as the spirit of a place:

> A poet of spiderwort and jacks-in-the-pulpit,
> hollyhocks against the toolshed.
> An unsmiling dark blond.
> I dug up protected and private things.
> That sort, I was.
> My graves went undecorated and my churches
> abandoned. This wasn't planned, but practice. (73)

Unearthing, deconsecrating, telling secrets, migrating in time, growing like a weed, the poet and her language retain their power by remaining attached to this place, "the poet of good walking shoes — a necessity/ in vernacular parts" (73–74).

Now if poets all over the place, from the past 250 years if not much longer ago, use signs of place as ways to organize poems we would now call lyric, what's special about Wright? Why is she not just one more case of a claim about place and poetry generally? One answer is that she knows that's what she does, that she concentrates on it, at least in *String Light*: another answer is that her style emphasizes dialect words and usages, aural effects and sociolinguistic markers, so that the language of the poem (not just the things she says she sees) speaks to the particular set of people who live in that place (a claim that does not hold, for example, in Housman, though of course it does in Burns).

But a more important answer is this: Wright, as all her critics notice, learned both from the image-centered, emotive poetics of the late 1960s and 1970s — from James Wright, from W. S. Merwin — and from the language writing she encountered once she moved to San Francisco. Wright can highlight ways that lyric can use place because her lyric poems strip other means and kinds of coherence away. We can see her using signs of locality, language about place and place-attachment, as ways to organize a poem where other kinds of expectation and organization — consistency of scene or speaking voice, for example, or narrative causality, or tonal unity — have been deliberately kept out. We do not always know what has happened or who did what to whom — but we know where we are.

Wright appeals to place when other means of coherence have failed. But such appeals have their own history too. As John MacKay has explained, writers — in and out of lyric poetry — have appealed to a sense of place as a refuge from theory, any theory, theory as such. "The periodic discrediting of rational-theoretical frameworks," MacKay writes, "perhaps leading in radical instances to the invalidation of frameworks per se, might lead to a search for immanent meanings or for particularity beyond significance: in landscapes, in nature, in the 'mutely' objective," so that the sense of "place . . . resists replacement by stubbornly asserting, if not accounting for, its own specialness" (57). MacKay has been writing about Shelley's "Mont Blanc," but his sentence could apply with equal justice to "Tintern Abbey," to "Song for the Rainy Season," to "The Ozark Odes," to Basil Bunting's *Briggflatts*, or indeed to Mary Dalton's *Merrybegot*, on which more soon. What is for MacKay's Shelley a matter of poetic theory — of ideas that the poem tries to explain — becomes for Wright a principle of technique.

Wright concludes *String Light* with "The Ozark Odes," sixteen poems — most under ten lines — devoted first and last to the spirit of the place. One just lists "Arkansas Towns," Acorn to Zent, one line per poem: in her Ozarks some place names have a kind of Cratylic function, where the name assumes the nature of the thing. Wright's unusual word choice — her use of words that strike her as proper, outsiders as common, nouns — also points to the difference between language use within, and outside, a local community. But Wright's sense of place does not grow from diction alone. The first of "The Ozark Odes" is "Lake Return":

> Maybe you have to be from there to hear it sing:
> Give me your waterweeds, your nipples,
> your shoehorn and your four-year letter jacket,
> the molded leftovers from the singed pot.
> Now let me see your underside, white as fishes.
> I lower my gaze against your clitoral light. (94)

Do you have to be from there, or can you go there through Wright's language? Can she take us there? It is a question not just about the Ozarks but about the efficacy of Grossman's "departicularized" voice of lyric in general, which aspires to make present one person's experience for someone else, somewhere else. Wright's rhetorical device here is something akin to apophasis: saying you cannot do something while trusting the audience to know that it's what you just did.

But what sings in Wright's five-beat, not-quite-blank verse? It is akin to America, a place of welcome, but a place of idiosyncrasy. "Give me" alludes to Emma Lazarus, and suggests that the lake, not the poet, speaks. All sorts of things turn up in this lake, things from the past, years ago or perhaps last night; it's a place for sex, a place for the feminine too. There is a real Lake Return, west of Harrison, Arkansas; you can catch bass there. The lake is also, for Wright, a place

C. D. Wright (1949–)

for the return of the repressed, a place for memory, a place for effects that deny clear explanation: it is, in fact, a place for lyric itself. Lyric, the personal, the useless, the ultimately inexplicable, the sexy, the charming, the weird and also the feminine: that's what you find when you return to the lake, where the poet has made herself a kind of ineffective fishing guide. (Whatever you catch, it's not something you eat.)

And then there is the final, two-line poem, also called "Lake Return": "Why I come here: need for a bottom, something to refer to;/ where all things visible and invisible commence to swarm" (98).

The slightly archaic diction, and then the twang, the sense that a story will start (and then, no story), the way that each term points to multiple claims about where she is and who she can be, the jokes embedded in the sublimity — all these are effects by which we recognize Wright. Here those effects serve the place, serve the argument that her poems have made about the place: it (both "the Ozarks" in general, and this lake in particular) have become a place from which she can speak, a foundation for the verbal connections that would otherwise lack common reference, that would have no place to start, and nowhere to return.

"Place," writes the philosopher Edward Casey, paraphrasing Aristotle, "has the power to make things be *somewhere*. . . . Without place things would not only fail to be located; they would not even be *things*: they would have *no place to be the things they are*" (*Fate* 71). A threat to place is "ontological"; it threatens "a loss in a *kind* of being and not merely in the number of beings that exist" (*Fate* 71). Place, for Casey and other philosophical writers in this vein (they follow, in some ways, Heidegger and Bergson) stands against space, because it is not (as "space" is) measurable, quantifiable, observer-independent. Yet place also stands against the purely inner, the invisible and intangible: it is a kind of shared space or transitional zone between the outer and the inner worlds, between things that are no part of us, that are not experience, and experience too inward to be shared.

No wonder, then, that so much poetry wants to be like place, and to use aspects of place, when it can, and to use them the more when other mediating factors, such as narrative and religious or social purpose, do not work well. And this way of using place in poetry — which we have seen in Wright, in Niedecker, in Whitman — works across kinds of places: wild or tame; urban, rural, wilderness, or suburb; with, or without, the explicit purpose of constructing an ecological ethics that has figured in other critics' attention to place (a purpose I endorse, but cannot follow here).

But there are other philosophers, other theories of place and emplacement, out there. So far I have been working, tacitly and explicitly, within a tradition of phenomenology as it borders on geography, with thinkers from several disciplines — Casey (and, behind him, Heidegger) in philosophy, Kevin Lynch in urban planning, Tony Hiss in *The Experience of Place* — who want to know what it's like to be somewhere. There is another tradition of thinking about place, a tradition sometimes called critical geography. This more or less Marxist line of thought, associated with Henri Lefebvre, David Harvey and Doreen Massey, among others, shows how our sense of place has changed, and how that sense depends on social systems that move us along from place to place, against our own interests or in the interests of capital. Writers in this tradition emphasize what Jules Boykoff, in an essay called "Poets as Experimental Geographers," calls "a processual definition of place" — place is not just turf, and the sense of place is not a static attachment, a taproot in history (228). "Instead, place is conceived as a complex tapestry of perpetually emergent story, a congregation of 'throwntogetherness' rather than a coherent, fixed patch of land" (228).

This story — and the other stories each story leaves out — are Spahr's subject in *Well Then There Now*, in Hawai'i, in Ohio, on the high seas. Ian Davidson has found in other contemporary poets other embodiments for the new critical geography: these poets resist, as Spahr does, both the way that neo-liberal capital tries to move us around arbitrarily (to replace "place" with "space") and the older sense of rootedness that phenomenology and poetry, tied to an old sense of "place," can imply. Heideggerians tend to emphasize place as rootedness, or as a way to feel at home: critical geographers, and the poets who follow them, resist that feeling. "In an increasingly spatialized world," Davidson says, "notions of place have to change," and "so too will notions of poetry" (31).

They will, but perhaps not as much as Davidson thinks. His poets — from Ed Dorn to J. H. Prynne — "question the notion that the poem can capture . . . the 'true spirit' of a place and an identity that exists prior to and outside the poem and is expressed by the poem" (60). They pursue a postmodern "shift from an interest in ideas of place to an interest in the constructed nature of space," and in "the alienation and dislocation of an increasingly spatialized post-modern America" (and, he goes on to show, postmodern Britain) (70). I do not disagree. Instead I have been trying to identify the thesis to which Davidson's arguments provide antitheses, and to show that some poets, Spahr among them, include both thesis and antithesis in the same poem.

Another such poet — one that Davidson also favors — is Frank

Frank O'Hara (1926–1966)

O'Hara: "If I rest for a moment near The Equestrian/ pausing for a liver sausage sandwich in the Mayflower Shoppe" — so his poem "Music" begins — "that angel seems to be leading the horse into Bergdorf's/ and I am naked as a table cloth, my nerves humming" (1). The phrases both jar and charm — they suggest dislocation and flux; they also suggest public nudity (which stands, by the end of the poem, for being without cash). The modern city has certainly been "constructed," and by capitalism too: the intersection where "Music" appears to take place, the southeastern corner of Central Park, is now and was then among the most expensive spots of commercial real estate in North America. But O'Hara also invites us — as Wright did — to go there with him, to see the sights, to enjoy it, to find it amusing, and to see whether we recognize the proper nouns: Bergdorf Goodman, 754 Fifth Avenue, is still there.

I have been trying to demonstrate that the sense of place as such, the genius loci, can remain central to memorable poetry, to poetry that counts as lyric, in the 21st century as well as the 18th, whether or not that poetry participates in other contemporary projects, for example, mapping the dislocations of capitalism, or foregoing consistent narrative and point of view. Where critics in Davidson's tradition emphasize rupture, I have been identifying continuity, trying to show what resources from the past are available now.

I have also been trying to disentangle what seem to be outmoded, or very limited, Romantic or Heideggerian notions of at-home-ness, of rootedness, from the much more capacious set of ways in which poems can invite us to stand with the poet, to imagine ourselves with the poet, in a particular place, here and now. A poetry of place need not be a poetry of one place, nor even of home. Elise Partridge spent her early years on the East Coast of the United States, but made her poetic career in British Columbia. One of the pleasures of rereading her late work is the way that her poems show how attention to place, to the feeling of being rooted in a place, does not preclude migration from one place to another: at the end of her poem "Dislocations," one

starling's heritage
may have been to nibble dropped brioches
in the Tuileries, but
look at her now, making a virtue of necessity
with a bag of cheese curls in the Bronx.

Already you're a hybrid,
you feel your strengths intermingling
like rivers braiding,
you're startled as the young tree
that suddenly keeps finding peaches at the end of its limbs. (51)

Partridge may have had in mind Yeats's prayer that his daughter remain "rooted in one dear perpetual place" (*Poems* 189). Her poem of irregular assonance answers him by saying that you can move from one place to another, like a starling, and still find spiritual nourishment: you can re-attune yourself and your poems, becoming — in Yeats's terms — unexpectedly fruitful, as if you had become a new kind of tree. (Starlings were introduced to North America in the late 19th century, like villanelles.)

Casey adds that for Gaston Bachelard, as for other thinkers in the phenomenological tradition, "to come to terms with the inner life, it is not enough to constitute a biography or autobiography in narrative terms; one must also, and more crucially, do a topoanalysis of the places one has inhabited or experienced" (*Fate* 289). *Must* seems too strong, but we *can*: that topoanalysis can be a job fit for poems. The experience of a lyric poem is like the experience of place, both shared and inward, and so lyric poems can both emulate and perform that topoanalysis. We might even say that our prior experience of place, both shared (other people can stand where we stand) and inward (unquantifiable, subjective), helps a poet suggest to us that the shared inwardness of a poem (of, say, "Crossing Brooklyn Ferry," or "Dislocation") is real, not just a word game, not a fraud.

Nor does a place — in order to provoke, or produce, a poem — have to feel like home. Nicholas Bradley writes that "the idea of

Elise Partridge (1958–2015)

sense of place usually presupposes that the poet, whose identity is seen to be contiguous with that of the lyric speaker, is intimately familiar with the location concerned, often to the extent that it provokes visceral responses, as in Wordsworth's remembrance of Tintern Abbey," or rather of the woods and hills a few miles upstream from the abbey (157). Wordsworth writes of another wild place, in his "Poems on the Naming of Places": "Soon did that spot become my *other* home" (emphasis mine) (200). But Wordsworth's are not the only available ways to write a poem attuned to a place. You can write a poem about a place that struck you on a brief jaunt, whether or not it became your "other home," or about a place where you settled as an adult (Frank O'Hara did not grow up in New York). You can write about a place where you feel out of place, as in Wallace

Stevens's "Farewell to Florida," or about a place you want to leave, as in Louis MacNeice's magnificently bitter "Valediction," about moving permanently away from Ireland, or about a place to which your connection seems comically minimal, as in Elizabeth Bishop's "Arrival at Santos" or Elizabeth Alexander's poem beginning "I could go to any city/ and write a poem, so here/ I am in Miami" (48).

And what is unfamiliar in a place — whether you go there, or whether you just read about it — depends on what already seems familiar, to the implicit reader or to the implied author and her representative within the poem. Does the poem address fellow inhabitants of the place, or outsiders? Does it assume that we already know the place? Where is Bergdorf Goodman? Where is Port-of-Spain? Where is the Wye? Where is Adlestrop (more on that place later, too)? Or does it presume to introduce that place to outsiders? Does it present somebody who grew up there, who looks back on what happened to her, diachronically, or does it address the place once, synchronically, now? Is the place seen in close-up (as in most of Bishop's "Jeronimo's House") or in the context of the larger political or architectural or climatological region (as at the end of the poem, with its final word "hurricane")? (26) How does the poem situate its readers, in space and in time, as it orients — or re-orients, or disorients — the poet to this place? How does it evoke (as Davidson wants contemporary poems to evoke) disorientation?

All texts about place raise these questions, but poetry tends to answer them line by line, or word by word. In some poems ("Lines Composed a Few Miles Above Tintern Abbey," for example) the answers to all these questions change between the beginning and the end; and to track changes in a poem's relationship to place is also to track the changes in what sort of person the poem lets us meet, what sort of people we see in the "flood-tide" below.

We may see dead people. Eighteenth-century poems that seem lyric, or pre-Romantic, to us tend also to be poems about place; surprisingly often they are poems about graves (such as Gray's "Elegy Written in a Country Church Yard"). We might say that "Tintern

"Elegy Written in a Country Church Yard" by Thomas Gray.

Abbey" makes its wild site a grave site for several of Wordsworth's past selves. Geoffrey Hartman, whom I may well have been following all along, noticed decades ago the "merging of epitaph and nature poetry" in Wordsworth's earliest characteristic poems: he found and grew them together out of the heretofore minor genre of the inscription (as in "Lines Left Upon a Seat in a Yew Tree"), a genre that Wordsworth made into a freestanding kind of poem (211, 221). "The new poetry projects a sacred marriage: that of the poet's genius with the genius loci," and "merging . . . the poet's spirit with spirit of place" (322). (Hartman was writing there about Collins and Gray; he might have added the Wartons, and Charlotte Smith.) It's no accident that "elegy" becomes subsumed into "lyric" (as Alastair Fowler has argued) and both into "poetry" generally — gradually, by fits and starts — over the same decades, let's say 1770 to 1910, in which the locodescriptive poem becomes a norm.

In a poem about a graveyard or a burial site these processes take place at once, each supporting another — you can follow them all along these lines from Gray and Warton to Larkin's "Church-Going," or Hughes's "Harlem," or Williams's "The Yachts." Partridge made a poem from her notes on Robert Lowell's lecture about Williams's poems: "The yachts here could be women, thoroughbreds," she has Lowell saying, "anything beautiful trampling over all/ it doesn't notice" (37). You could be walking on their graves. We might say, in a de Manian mood, that all places used as sites for supposedly lyric poems (poems in which people are "departicularized") become graveyards. Yet we might also associate such graves, once put into poems, once described *as* places *in* poems, with life itself, and with the resurrection of the dead.

But if the lyric of place descends from the graveyard poem, it can also encompass other sub-genres: for example, prothalamia. You can see yourself in a place so enthusiastically that you want to get married there, or to marry the place itself. Wallace Stevens envisioned that kind of marriage but could not dramatize it: the "mystic marriage" of Captain Bawda, in *Notes Toward a Supreme Fiction*, which works because both parties love their island place, is not exactly a marriage that works out in much of his verse, where local belonging, in Connecticut or Pennsylvania, requires less festive terms. The contemporary American poet Aracelis Girmay, on the other hand, writes a successful, brief prothalamion of place in her poem "Noche de Lluvia, San Salvador":

> Rain who nails the earth,
> whose infinite legs
> nail the earth, whose silver faces
> touch my faces, I marry you. & open
> all the windows of my house to hear
> your million feral versions
> of si si
>
> sí
>
> si
>
> si (36)

Girmay dissolves into onomatopoetic affirmation as if she were getting married to all the raindrops at once, and as if they could marry (establish a lasting union with) the land: the poetic line dissolves into open form, almost into visual mimesis ("s" and accented "i" like slant lines made by rain) as the bilingual poet — an American and a New Yorker in a Spanish-speaking tropical capital — vanishes into what she hears and sees.

Whether it makes its place into a kind of graveyard, or a consecrated marriage spot, a home, a playground, or a public square, a poem of topoanalysis makes its place over again as a place for a soul, a place of resurrection, where a spirit comes to life again. Consecrated, emotionally bound, to the place (whether or not it is, as Yeats preferred, "one dear perpetual place"), the poem is like a ceremony, or a magic circle, for a disenchanted time. That is one way to read a number of the poems that I have already discussed — Wright's Ozark Odes, O'Hara's "Music," Girmay's prothalamion, Niedecker's reminiscence of stones. It is also one way to read, for example, John Donne's "The Relic," though "The Relic" does not name (outside the London-based satires, Donne's poems rarely name) one place. It is one way to read Rilke's "Der Panther," explicitly set in the Jardin des Plantes. It is also one way to read Randall Jarrell's great poem of liberation from the body, "The Woman at the Washington Zoo" (indebted to Rilke's panther). Jarrell's poem does name a particular place — it is a poem of emplacement and a lyric poem and a prison poem: "O bars of my own body, open, open!" the Woman exclaims, inspired as well as intimidated by the leopard, the vulture, and the colorful foreign women who come together thanks to the particular mission of Washington, D.C.'s National Zoo: "The saris go by me from the embassies.// Cloth from the moon. Cloth from another planet./ They look back at the leopard like the leopard" (215).

There's a lot more to say about Washington, D.C., in poetry — in Whitman's poetry, and in Jarrell's, and in Alexander's, and in the poetry of my own contemporaries, and if I were speaking in Washington, D.C., I might end with that. Instead, I will end in

Randall Jarrell (1914–1965)

Newfoundland. Before going there, though, I want to introduce one more distinction between ways of representing place, or rather between two senses of "place," both of which a poem can represent: one sense is literally larger than the other. We can imagine many concentric or concurrent kinds of sense of place, from continent to city to square meter, but the distinction I want to notice in poetic language requires two, and only two, kinds: one I'll have to call "region" (though the word has of course meant many other things, especially in Canada); the other I'll call "locus."

Region here means an area, whether historical or hydrological or linguistic ("the Colorado River watershed"; Alberta; Gloucestershire; the Gaeltacht) defined by shared characteristics that extend beyond what the senses can know first-hand: it can be as large as a continent or as small as a residential neighborhood. Locus is defined and bounded by the potential first-hand experience of one person in one place, whether she walks or stands still: a tree there, a brick building here, the scent of one tree or one store, a near or far horizon. Locus is something we can stand in or move through; region, usually, does not change as we move — you can walk from block to block and remain in Brooklyn, or from grove to grove and remain in the same forest. Washington, D.C., is a region; the terrace for tourists in front of the leopard cage at the National Zoo is a locus. When we think about where we are, we think about both locus and region, a process that Casey calls "double-tracking" (*Getting* 278).

Every locus occupies more than one region (58th and Fifth, Manhattan, New York, the Hudson River watershed, and so on); a region can be political (defined by human geography) or physical (defined by water, climate, fauna, and so on). All poems about identifiable places evoke both locus and region, though they can focus on one or the other, or shift from one to another within the poem. Edward Thomas's "Adlestrop," for example, begins with a moment on a railway platform and ends by evoking the habitats of birds all over "Oxfordshire and Gloucestershire" — the poet disturbed by the locus, brought up short (in short, disconnected, *portato* sentences) at an unfamiliar station, ends up magnificently consoled as birdsong and hayricks ground him in his region (35).

We might even say that the interaction of region and locus constitutes our sense of place. But they tend to inform poetry in different ways. Very often, but not always, they inform different aspects of poetic technique. Region — my final hypothesis about the poetry of place says — tends to show up in diction, since when you bring a notable word into a poem you are pointing to the ways in which that word has already been used. As Deborah Cameron explained in a previous Sedgewick lecture, "clustering linguistic features together into a culturally recognizable style becomes the outward and audible sign of membership in an imagined community" (23). The features easiest to "cluster" are the features that can be collected or mentally tabulated most easily — that is, words. Rare words can tell us what kind of rare features characterize the physical landscape, recurring farther than the eye can see; dialect words can tell us who is speaking, corresponding to weather or physical place but also to human geography. And specialized words show familiarity with the region, with the kind of rock formation or the species of fauna or the names of Ozark towns. Conversely, if you don't feel at home in the place, you may note that you don't know the names of the animals, as Elise Partridge did in her inviting poem called "Everglades," in which "a bird swaying on a coral-bean/ sang two notes that might have been 'Name me'" (3).

Syntax and line shape, on the other hand, tend to match the way poems depict locus, the shape of a site from minute to minute, as the poet — and hence the reader — experience it first-hand. Syntax and line are the shapes that the poem makes in time, and they can match the track of a walker, or the saccade of the eye, orienting itself to the horizon or the view, to the new surround. "The eye is the first circle," wrote Ralph Waldo Emerson; "the horizon which it forms is the second," and the poetic line — as my colleague Elisa New has explained in her book *The Line's Eye* — can trope the distance between them (403). The singular sentence can imitate paths through space, and its syntax *can* (though it need not) match the shape of the place: intricate and crowded for a dense city block, flat and clear when we stand on a plain. Syntax, accreting or altering sense over time, stands for and in turn helps build what the philosopher David Seamon calls a "lifeworld," a mental space through which bodily "action unfolds" (12).

I have argued that place provides a profound occasion for poetry across schools, styles, continents and centuries, even before the Romantics, and certainly afterwards; I have argued that place can do so, for the kinds of poems we now call lyric, because the contemplation of place is one way in which the "outside," what's shared, potentially public, accessible to more than one person at once, can seem to meet the "inside," the private or individual experience that we may consider ultimately unknowable (unless it is our own) and yet expect poetry to reproduce. I have shown — I hope I have shown — how this connection between the outside and the inside, the knowable and the inwardly unknown, not only encourages poets to make poems from places, but makes certain kinds of places especially important: graveyards, for example, and prisons, and also places that feel like home.

Finally I have claimed that two aspects of poetic technique fit two parts of our experience of place: diction for region, and syntax for locus. That is not a hard and fast rule but it is a hypothesis confirmed by some (only some) of the poets most invested in place. Wright is one: I think that Wordsworth (who uses north of England words where he can — "force" for "waterfall," for example) might be another, and I am certain that Mary Dalton is a third. Diction evokes both human geography (dialect words) and physical geography (names for special features of land and sea) almost throughout Mary Dalton's exceptional book *Merrybegot*, whose short poems about Newfoundland people incorporate many Newfoundland dialect words, most of them in the Dictionary of Newfoundland English, first prepared in 1982 and placed online in 1998–99. Dalton has arranged the words to fit her anecdotes and her characters' movements through physical space (their locus), as well as to fit their points of view. At the end of "Bridesboys," for example, young men throwing a pre-wedding party go too far: they make

> A racket out on the bridge —
> Up she went like a brindy bough,
> And the father, stiff as brewis,
> Come out and drove us off out of it,
> And the water barrels upsot, the
> Bride cake made away with.
> The day after, a big kick-up.
> We were all mops and brooms.
> Small chance he'll have us in for a
> Piece of the groaning cake
> Come fall. (14)

"Brindy" can mean either "red-brown" or "angry," like the standard English "fiery": "brindy bough" is a DNE example. Apparently a party got out of hand until the bride's father shut it down: his demeanor reminds Dalton's speaker of "brewis," hardtack or soup made from hardtack. The variant spelling "upsot" also comes from the DNE, in the entry for "bridesboys": "That's all we got out of the wedding — upsot the water barrels, made away with the bride-cake and hove feathers everywhere."

Once you see the regional function of diction in Dalton, you can hear the locative, time-bound, place-making function of syntax and line. Syntax follows these "bridesboys," who speak collectively, off the bridge (one consonant away from "bride"), and into the cleanup the following morning. It then leads them out of the poem: they're not going to be invited back for the "groaning cake," served after a birth, "Come the fall." (The wedding has not yet taken place, but the bridesboys already know when the baby is due.) Diction establishes membership in a community that shares a physical environment (they live "up and down the harbor"); syntax moves the smaller group of first-person plural figures up the bridge.

Let's look at a simpler poem with a first-person singular speaker, another poem whose title appears in the DNE: "Cullage," inferior fish or food made from the fish. Dalton's fisherman catches nothing else, and isn't happy:

> Not a bit of drite.
> Day after day of this mauzy old stuff —
> Now the fish is maggoty and it's slimy,
> And I got to get out on the flake again
> With small tubs and pickle and wash it.
> And rewash it and perhaps the weather'll
> Marl on like this for a fortnight,
> And when 'tis all over I got nothing —
> Nothing to show but a mess of cullage. (23)

The words tell us what kind of place we are in as well as who lives there: the syntax and pace tell us where this person is, now.

Fish "flakes" used by fishermen to dry their cod are an important aspect of Newfoundland culture.

"Drite" (related to "drought") is dryness: the humid weather makes it nigh impossible to preserve or cure caught fish. "Mauzy" means misty or foggy: the sad fisherman moves backwards and forwards through time and space, and he keeps coming back to his "flake," an old-fashioned, low-tech platform for curing cod. The words tell us where we are, in general, who speaks and who might be listening — they set a region: the shape of the sentence gives us the speaker's movement, in this case his fruitless back-and-forth movement, through time and space, ending on "nothing," "nothing," not even a mess of pottage, like the hunter Esau, but a poor fisherman's half-rhyme for it, "cullage."

Dalton is hardly the first poet to write about Newfoundland, though she may be the first to use the Dictionary of Newfoundland English this way. Earlier poets of Newfoundland had, of course, tried to present what (in their view) distinguished the island, the region, and its people: writers from elsewhere noted "the distinctive accents, idiom, songs, and proverbs of Newfoundlanders" (so Patrick O'Flaherty writes) as early as 1794 (88). A skeptical reader might ask whether Dalton's poems about, and in, Newfoundland English paint inappropriately sunny pictures of outport lives, whether her poems are like tourist products for outsiders; I raise the question largely to note that Paul Chafe of Memorial University has answered it, explaining at some length how *Merrybegot* uses dialect to present, not a singular, misleading fiction about a unified, vanishing culture, but a set of realistically imagined "individuals negotiating their own space" (1).

It is far from my place to say whether, or how closely, Dalton's ventriloquism reflects recent or present-day outport life. But it is certainly my place, and my pleasure, as a poetry critic who grew up far away from all the people Dalton describes, to appreciate her technique, to show how it resonates far from her home (as Wordsworth's, and Niedecker's, and Wright's, and Girmay's, ought to resonate far from theirs), and to show how the choices she makes about diction and syntax, about dialect and about sentence shape, make use of both region and locus, and make her poems sing.

Like many poems — Wright's among them — that make heavy use of dialect, Dalton's verse in *Merrybegot* is ambivalently elegiac. These old ways, and the old diction that goes with them — "janneying" for mumming (35); mumming itself; the building of flakes — did not make the island a paradise. But they set the community apart; some of them might be going, though they are not gone. The poems are pointedly not graveyard poems, but they are poems of memory, memory fixed on land: and the sea that threatens and nourishes all the folkways and all the people in Dalton's poetry also threatens to take all their words away. To keep using the words is to stay attached to the place: but to move through the place (the region) within *Merrybegot* is to move from person to person, from place to place, with consistency provided by the diction, variety by story and by syntax.

One more short poem of Dalton's can show, I think, how a sense of place lets modern poets orient ourselves towards a shared

Mary Dalton (1950–)

experience, something "inside" (subjective) but also "outside"; how poems on place use both region and locus, both physical and human geography; how a sense of place hooks together what might seem like separate sub-genres of lyric (in this case, the Christmas poem, the scenic meditation, the elegy); how the persistence, and the continued availability, of place seems to work against the passage of time; and how syntax tracks locus (where the poet herself could be and will go), while diction tracks region (what kind of place we are in, and who tends to live there). The poem is "Mat," and the title — while not a dialect word exactly — turns up in the DNE, because it denotes a Newfoundland practice, the making of hooked rugs:

> Some of them could go fast as the wind —
> Nell now — and she was a great hand at it,
> Scrolls and squares and dogs and roses
> And one time a red punt on the water.

And then the scrubbing —
Dragging mats down to the cove in summer,
We beat them against the beach rocks,
And the salt water gave back their colour.
And come Christmas
Out we went mummering,
Out in the fools, happy as kings,
Mat rags sewed into our clothes. (42)

Unlike, say, "Bridesboys," "Mat" does not flaunt words that exist only in the DNE: instead it makes the textiles and the representations they contain into figures for the poems, which aspire to sound as insistently local as the mats look, and it puts common words into their Newfoundland usages (Dalton's most recent work as of 2015 is a book of centos entitled *Hooking*, comparing her verbal bricolage to the mats of traditional craft). "Them" must refer to makers of mats, though the sentence could almost apply to ships, as if the mats could be sails: the human geography of dialect words implies the physical geography of the landscape the poems reproduce.

Again, Dalton has used a DNE sample: "'Twas hooked with rags, condemned rags, and they had a proper mat hook. Some o' them could go as fast as the wind," attributed to a taped interview: the sense of region comes from the sounds as well as the choice of words. But the sense of space that her characters move through comes from the syntax, which does move fast, as if out on the water. Those characters take "mats down to the cove in summer," connecting themselves to their inlet, their way to the sea. By Christmas, the mats have changed their function again: rags that would go to make mats are "sewed into our clothes" as "we" — that is, the women, the matmakers — go "out in the fools," that is, dressed up as the Christmas mummers called "the Fools" (with the article) who became, the DNE says, a rowdy Newfoundland "institution."

Are poets fools, too? Are they kings of infinite space, or lords of misrule? Is there something ridiculous in trying to preserve or represent the ineffable self with words? If so, it is no more ridiculous than trying to carry into the present day and trying to represent — for those outside the place — the traditions that tie a community to that place: and that is the representation that *Merrybegot* performs. The women are makers, poets, who start by connecting abstract lines and then depict things, like a "red punt on the water" (Dalton's next book would be *Red Ledger*). These women, the poet's allies, have refreshed themselves and their textiles with, literally, local color — "the salt water gave back their colour" could be a slogan for Dalton's entire book. These mats are to rags as Dalton's poems are to words, and both mats and poems become ways to celebrate a connection to the place that belongs to the poet but does not belong to the poet alone.

"A place," as Davidson points out, "is identified through its relationship to other places," at least in language (89). What we talk about when we talk about San Francisco is going to differ depending on whether we are comparing it to (or describing it to somebody who has come from) Vancouver or San Diego or a small town in

Elizabeth Bishop (1911–1979)

Arkansas or New York. And yet it does not follow (as Davidson implies) that we cannot try to embody a single place in memorable language: place "is unstable" (89) but less so than many other concepts (for example, anger, or desire, or God) that also appear in verse. And Mary Dalton's poetry is exceptional, not just in terms of its memorable qualities but in terms of the *degree* of its relationship to place.

Like Wright, and for that matter like Housman, Dalton is writing both for people who can say, as Elizabeth Bishop says, "I recognize the place, I know it!" and for people who come to the place through her poems; for people from elsewhere, as well as for people who are, or are from, there (165). Social researchers, as well as nonfiction writers, have demonstrated that you don't have to stay in one place, nor limit yourself to one place, in order to experience attachment to a place — "places matter to people and place attachment is associated with life satisfaction" even among people and in social strata where it is normal to move — although "those who are mobile may perceive places as meaningful for different reasons, and develop different types of attachment, than long-term residents," concludes the sociologist Per Gustafson (38). We can, like Wright or like Bishop or like Elise Partridge, "develop and sustain attachments to several different places," as Gustafson's interview-based research confirms (40). And those attachments remain or even *become* available as subjects in lyric poems. Dalton's Newfoundland, like Wright's Ozarks, like O'Hara's Manhattan for that matter, and like Whitman's ferry, does not assume but demonstrates how a poem about a place can bring together, can show something in common, for people far away from one another, and from the poet, in time or space.

Maybe you don't have to be from there to hear it sing — not if "it" is a place, not if it's in a poem. Or maybe Dalton's poetry demonstrates the way that the resources of poetry link the inside with the outside, the apparently unique experience with a sense of place that can, in principle, be shared. And maybe you don't have to go to a place whose language is as exceptional as Newfoundland English, nor to a place that's world-famous (say, O'Hara's New York), nor to a place identified with nostalgia (say, Adlestrop), in order to see those effects: is there a poetry of particular suburbs? of "the suburbs" (as Jo Gill's recent book argues)? of virtual place on the Internet (as Gabby Bess and other twentysomething poets suggest)? That is a project for another place — but my provisional answer is somewhere between "Yes, there is" and "We'll see"; or maybe between "We're on our way" and "We're already there."

WORKS CITED

Alexander, Elizabeth. *The Venus Hottentot*. Charlottesville: University of Virginia Press, 1990.

Alexander, Neal, and David Cooper. *Poetry and Geography*. Liverpool: Liverpool University Press, 2013.

Altieri, Charles. "Sensibility, Rhetoric and Will: Some Tensions in Contemporary Poetry." *Contemporary Literature* 23:4 (1982): 451–79.

Auden, W. H. *Collected Poems*, ed. Edward Mendelson. New York: Vintage, 1991.

Barrell, John. *The Idea of Landscape and the Sense of Place, 1730–1840: An Approach to the Poetry of John Clare*. Cambridge: Cambridge University Press, 1972.

Beachy-Quick, Dan. *Wonderful Investigations: Essays, Meditations, Tales*. Minneapolis: Milkweed, 2012.

Bishop, Elizabeth. *Poems, Prose and Letters*, ed. Lloyd Schwartz and Robert Giroux. New York: Library of America, 2008.

Boyd, Brian. *Why Lyrics Last*. Cambridge, Mass.: Harvard University Press, 2012.

Boykoff, Jules. "Poets as Experimental Geographers." In Ian Davidson and Zoe Skoulding, eds., *Placing Poetry*. Amsterdam: Rodopi, 2013. 223–56.

Bradley, Nicholas. "The Fat Man on Snow Dome: Surprise and the Sense of Place (Or, Reading Laurie Ricou's David Wagoner)." *Western American Literature* 46:2 (2011): 116–41.

Cameron, Deborah. *More Heat than Light? Sex-difference Science & the Study of Language: The 2012 Garnett Sedgewick Memorial Lecture*. Vancouver: Ronsdale, 2012.

Casey, Edward P. *The Fate of Place*. Berkeley: University of California Press, 1997.

Casey, Edward P. *Getting Back Into Place*. Bloomington, In.: Indiana University Press, 1993.

Chafe, Paul. "Newfoundland Poetry as 'Ethnographic Salvage': Time, Place and Voice in the Poetry of Michael Crummey and Mary Dalton." *Studies in Canadian Literature/ Études en littérature canadienne* 32:2 (2007). Web.

Chaucer, Geoffrey. *The Canterbury Tales*, ed. V. A. Kolve and Glending Olson. New York: Norton, 2005.

Costello, Bonnie. *Shifting Ground: Reinventing Landscape in Modern American Poetry*. Cambridge, Mass.: Harvard University Press, 2003.

Creeley, Robert. *Collected Essays*. Berkeley: University of California Press, 1989.

Dalton, Mary. *Merrybegot*. Montreal: Signal/ Vehicule, 2003.

Davidson, Ian. *Ideas of Space in Contemporary Poetry*. London: Palgrave Macmillan, 2007.

Dictionary of Newfoundland English. St. John's: Memorial University. 1999 (1982). Web. http://www.heritage.nf.ca/dictionary/

Emerson, Ralph Waldo. *Essays and Lectures*, ed. Joel A. Porte. New York: Library of America, 1983.

Girmay, Aracelis. *Kingdom Animalia*. Rochester, N.Y.: BOA, 2011.

Grossman, Allen, with Mark Halliday. *The Sighted Singer*. Baltimore: Johns Hopkins University Press, 1992.

Gustafson, Per. "Place Attachment in an Age of Mobility." In Lynn C. Manzo and Patrick Devine-Wright, eds., *Place Attachment*. London: Routledge, 2014. 37–48.

Hartman, Geoffrey. *Beyond Formalism*. New Haven: Yale University Press, 1970.

Housman, A. E. *Collected Poems*. New York: Henry Holt, 1965.

Irmscher, Christoph. *Longfellow Redux*. Urbana: University of Illinois Press, 2006.

Jackson, Virginia, and Yopie Prins, eds. *The Lyric Theory Reader*. Baltimore: Johns Hopkins University Press, 2014.

Jarrell, Randall. *Complete Poems*. New York: Farrar, Straus and Giroux, 1969.

Johnson, Samuel. *Lives of the Poets, Vol. One*, ed. John H. Middendorf. New Haven: Yale University Press, 2010.

MacKay, John. *Inscription and Modernity: From Wordsworth to Mandelstam*. Bloomington, In.: Indiana University Press, 2006.

Niedecker, Lorine. *Lake Superior*. Seattle: Wave, 2013.

O'Flaherty, Patrick. *The Rock Observed: Studies in the Literature of Newfoundland*. Toronto: University of Toronto Press, 1979.

O'Hara, Frank. *Lunch Poems*. San Francisco: City Lights, 1964.

Partridge, Elise. *Chameleon Hours*. Chicago: University of Chicago Press, 2008.

Pound, Ezra. *The Cantos of Ezra Pound*. New York: New Directions, 1986 (1970).

Powell, Neil. "Dog Days." *PN Review* 208 (2012): 7–8.

Rich, Adrienne. *Later Poems Selected and New*. New York: Norton, 2012.

Seamon, David. "Place Attachment and Phenomenology." In Manzo and Devine-Wright, eds., *Place Attachment*. 11–22.

Shaw, Lytle. *Fieldworks*. Tuscaloosa: University of Alabama Press, 2013.

Spahr, Juliana. *Well Then There Now*. Jaffrey, N.H.: Godine/ Black Sparrow, 2011.

Stafford, Fiona. *Local Attachments*. Oxford: Oxford University Press, 2010.

Thomas, Edward. *Poems*. New York: Handsel, 2003.

Vendler, Helen. *Soul Says: On Recent Poetry*. Cambridge, Mass.: Harvard University Press, 1995.

Whitman, Walt. *Poetry and Prose*, ed. Justin Kaplan. New York: Library of America, 1982.

Williams, William Carlos. *Collected Poems Volume One*, ed. A. Walton Litz and Christopher MacGowan. New York: New Directions, 1986.

Williams, William Carlos. *Selected Essays*. New York: New Directions, 1969.

Wordsworth, William. *The Major Works*, ed. Stephen Gill. Oxford: Oxford University Press, 2008.

Wright, C. D. *Steal Away: Selected and New Poems*. Port Townsend, Wash.: Copper Canyon, 2002.

Yeats, W. B. *Essays and Introductions*. London: Macmillan, 1961.

Yeats, W. B. *Poems*, ed. Richard Finneran. Second ed. New York: Scribner, 1996.

ABOUT THE AUTHOR

STEPHEN BURT is professor of English at Harvard University and the author of several books of poetry and literary criticism, among them *Belmont* (2013); *The Art of the Sonnet*, with David Mikics (2010); *Close Calls with Nonsense: Reading New Poetry* (2009), a finalist for the National Book Critics Circle Award; *The Forms of Youth: 20th-Century Poetry and Adolescence* (2007); *Parallel Play* (2006); and *Randall Jarrell and His Age* (2002), winner of the Warren-Brooks Award for Literary Criticism. Burt's essays and reviews — most of them about poetry, some of them about comic books, gender, pop music, and other topics — have appeared in many journals, magazines and newspapers, including *American Literary History (ALH)*, *Boston Review*, the *London Review of Books*, *Modern Philology*, the *Nation*, and the *New York Times Book Review*.